This book belongs to:

_____

A catalogue record for this book is available from the British Library

Published by Ladybird Books Ltd
80 Strand WC2R 0RL
A Penguin Company

2 4 6 8 10 9 7 5 3 1
© LADYBIRD BOOKS LTD MMVII
LADYBIRD and the device of a Ladybird are trademarks of Ladybird Books Ltd

ISBN-13: 9781846465017
ISBN-10: 184646501X

Printed in Italy

Beauty and the Beast

illustrated by
Marsela Hajdinjak-Krec

Once there was a man
who had three daughters.
The youngest daughter
was called Beauty.
She was good and kind.

One day, the man had
to go away.
"Would you like me
to bring you back a
present?" he said to
his daughters.

6

"Please bring me back
a necklace," said the
first daughter.
"Please bring me back
a gold ring," said the
second daughter.
"Please bring me back
a rose," said Beauty.

The man got lost.
Then, he saw a castle.
The castle had roses
in the garden.

"I will bring back
these roses for Beauty,"
said the man.
"Do not take the roses!"
said a loud voice.
It was a Beast.

"Do not hurt me!"
said the man.
The Beast said, "I will
not hurt you. But you
must bring me back the
first thing you see when
you get home."

15

When the man got home, the first thing he saw was Beauty. Because she was good and kind, Beauty said, "I will go to live with the Beast."

The Beast was kind
to Beauty and Beauty
liked the Beast.
One day, the Beast
asked Beauty to marry
him. "No," said Beauty.
"I like you, but I will
not marry you."

19

One day, Beauty went
home to see her father.
When Beauty went
back to the castle,
the first thing she
saw was the Beast.
He was ill.

21

"Please do not be ill,"
Beauty said to the Beast.
"I *do* love you and
I *will* marry you."

Then, the Beast turned
into a handsome prince.
"Thank you for
breaking the spell,"
he said.

The handsome prince
asked Beauty to
marry him.
"Yes," said Beauty.
"I *do* love you and
I *will* marry you."

Read it yourself is a series of graded readers
designed to give young children a confident
and successful start to reading.

Level 2 is for children who are familiar with
some simple words and can read short
sentences. Each story in this level contains
frequently repeated phrases which help
children to read more fluently. Every page
in the story is accompanied by a detailed
illustration of the main action, which aids
understanding of the text and encourages
interest and enjoyment.

About this book

The story is told in a way which uses regular
repetition of the main words and phrases.
This enables children to recognise the words
more and more easily as they progress
through the book. An adult can help them to
do this by pointing at the first letter of each
word, and sometimes making the sound that
the letter makes. Children will probably need
less help as the story progresses.

*Beginner readers need plenty of help and
encouragement.*